Twelve Cowboys Ropin'

Susan Kralovansky

PELICAN PUBLISHING COMPANY

GRETNA 2015

by
Susan Holt Kralovansky

*The word "Pelican" and the depiction of a pelican are
trademarks of Pelican Publishing Company, Inc., and are
registered in the U.S. Patent and Trademark Office.*

Library of Congress Cataloging-in-Publication Data

Kralovansky, Susan Holt, author, illustrator.
  Twelve cowboys ropin' / by Susan Kralovansky.
     pages cm
  Summary: "In this Texas tale, each day begins with a gift from Pappy, ranging
from a mockingbird in a pecan tree to four prickly pears to twelve cowboys ro-
pin'"-- Provided by publisher.
  ISBN 978-1-4556-2081-4 (hardcover : alk. paper) -- ISBN 978-1-4556-2082-1
(e-book) [1. Stories in rhyme. 2. Texas--Fiction. 3. Counting.] I. Title. II. Title:
Twelve cowboys roping.
  PZ8.3.K8613Tw 2015
  [E]--dc23
                                        2014050029\

Printed in Malaysia

Published by Pelican Publishing Company, Inc.
1000 Burmaster Street, Gretna, Louisiana 70053

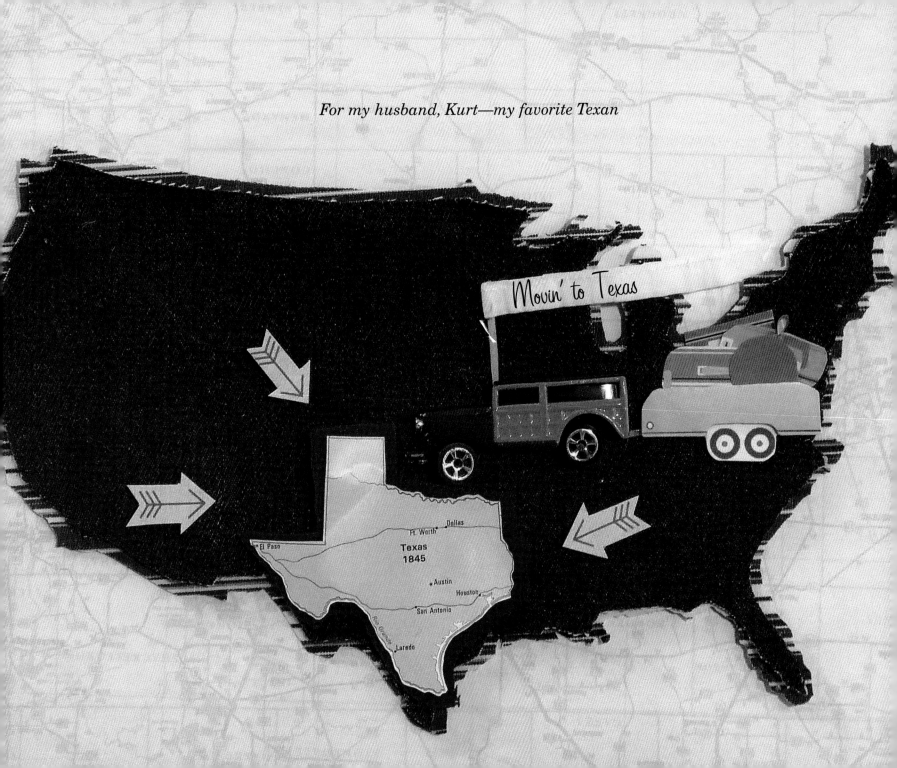

For my husband, Kurt—my favorite Texan

Movin' to Texas

Texas
1845

On my first day in Texas,
my pappy gave to me—
a mockingbird in a pecan tree.

On my second day in Texas,
my pappy gave to me—
two horny toads
and a mockingbird in a pecan tree.

On my third day in Texas,
my pappy gave to me—
three butterflies,
two horny toads,
and a mockingbird in a pecan tree.

On my fourth day in Texas,
my pappy gave to me—
four prickly pears,
three butterflies,
two horny toads,
and a mockingbird in a pecan tree.

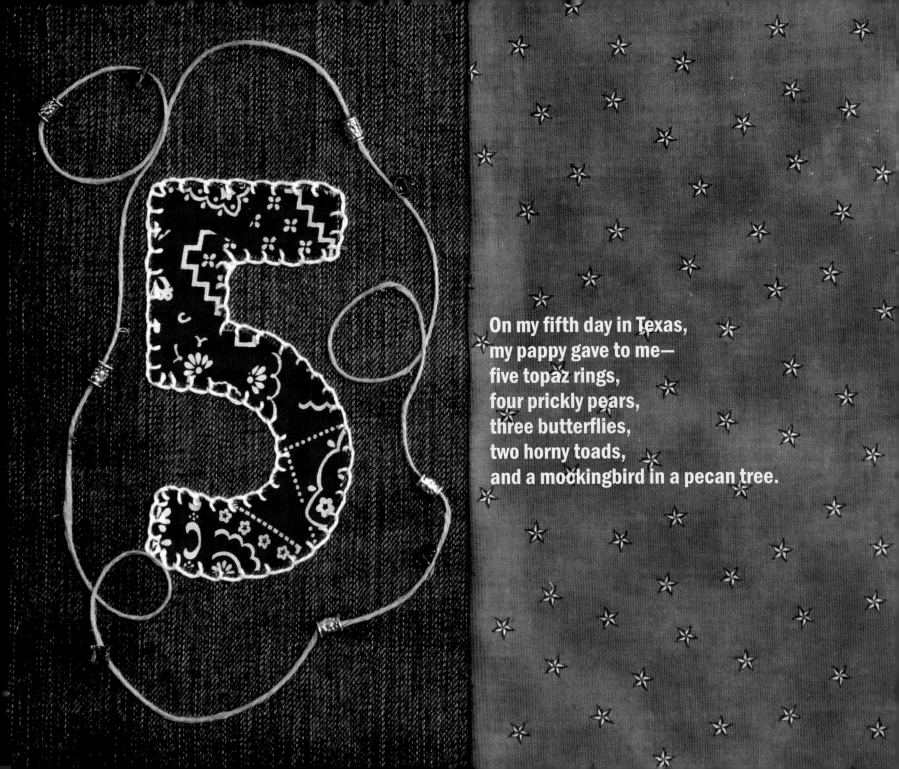

On my fifth day in Texas,
my pappy gave to me—
five topaz rings,
four prickly pears,
three butterflies,
two horny toads,
and a mockingbird in a pecan tree.

On my sixth day in Texas,
my pappy gave to me—
six longhorns grazin',
five topaz rings,
four prickly pears,
three butterflies,
two horny toads,
and a mockingbird in a pecan tree.

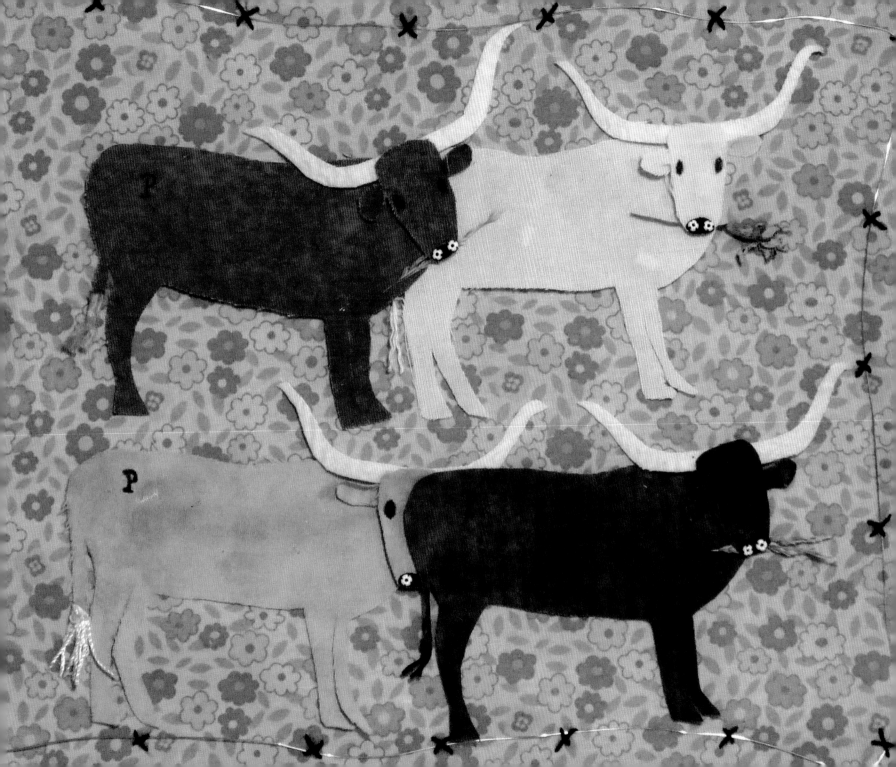

On my seventh day in Texas,
my pappy gave to me—
seven bats a-flyin',
six longhorns grazin',
five topaz rings,
four prickly pears,
three butterflies,
two horny toads,
and a mockingbird in a pecan tree.

On my eighth day in Texas,
my pappy gave to me—
eight dillos diggin',
seven bats a-flyin',
six longhorns grazin',
five topaz rings,
four prickly pears,
three butterflies,
two horny toads,
and a mockingbird in a pecan tree.

On my ninth day in Texas,
my pappy gave to me—
nine guitarists
strummin',
eight dillos diggin',
seven bats a-flyin',
six longhorns grazin',

five topaz rings,
four prickly pears,
three butterflies,
two horny toads,
and a mockingbird
in a pecan tree.

On my tenth day in Texas,
my pappy gave to me—
ten boots a-scootin',
nine guitarists strummin',
eight dillos diggin',
seven bats a-flyin',
six longhorns grazin',
five topaz rings,
four prickly pears,
three butterflies,
two horny toads,
and a mockingbird in a
pecan tree.

11

On my eleventh day in Texas,
my pappy gave to me—
eleven gals a-dancin',
ten boots a-scootin',
nine guitarists strummin',
eight dillos diggin',
seven bats a-flyin',
six longhorns grazin',
five topaz rings,
four prickly pears,
three butterflies,
two horny toads,
and a mockingbird in a
pecan tree.

On my twelfth day in Texas,
my pappy gave to me—
twelve cowboys ropin',
eleven gals a-dancin',
ten boots a-scootin',
nine guitarists strummin',
eight dillos diggin',
seven bats a-flyin',
six longhorns grazin',
five topaz rings,
four prickly pears,
three butterflies,
two horny toads,
and a mockingbird in a pecan tree.

Fun Facts

 Mockingbirds copy or "mock" other sounds. A mockingbird can sound like a bird, a dog, a tractor, a squeaky gate, and even a fire truck. The pecan tree was chosen as the official tree of Texas in 1919, and the pecan was adopted as the state health nut in 2001.

 When the Texas horned lizard or "horny toad" feels threatened, it flattens and freezes in place. Native Americans thought the horned lizard was a symbol of health and happiness.

 The monarch butterfly migrates when seasons change. Monarchs spend the winter months in Central Mexico. Then they fly to Texas in the spring.

 The prickly pear cactus has hair-like thorns instead of leaves. The sweet fruit of the cactus can be used to make jelly, syrup, and candy.

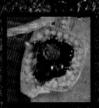 The Texas blue topaz is the state gemstone. The Lone Star Cut was named the state cut in 1977, and it shows a five-pointed star cut into a gemstone.

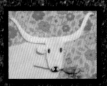 In 1995, Texas chose the longhorn as the official state large mammal. The name "longhorn" fits these animals. Some steers' horns grow to span seven feet!

 For nine months of the year, the Mexican free-tailed bats eat insects and live in caves, in deserted tunnels, and under bridges in Texas. They spend their winters in the south, just like the monarch butterfly.

 Nine-banded armadillos have bony plates of tough skin. An adult armadillo is about the size of a small cat.

 The guitar became the state instrument in 1997 because of its role in the musical history of Texas.

 The cowboy boot was named the official state footwear in 2007, thanks to the work of a Houston social studies teacher and her seventh-grade students.

 The square dance became the official folk dance of Texas in 1991.

 Many believe that the first rodeo took place in Pecos, Texas in 1883. A few cowboys met to find out who was the best at riding and roping.

Twelve Cowboys Ropin'

Traditional song with adapted lyrics by Susan Holt Kralovansky

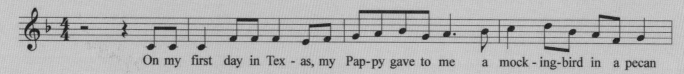

On my first day in Tex-as, my Pap-py gave to me a mock-ing-bird in a pecan

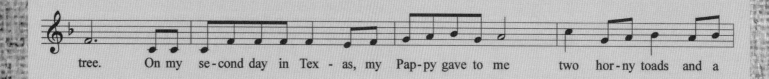

tree. On my se-cond day in Tex-as, my Pap-py gave to me two hor-ny toads and a

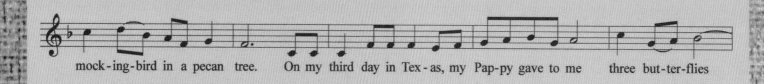

mock-ing-bird in a pecan tree. On my third day in Tex-as, my Pap-py gave to me three but-ter-flies

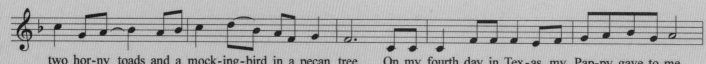

two hor-ny toads and a mock-ing-bird in a pecan tree. On my fourth day in Tex-as, my Pap-py gave to me

A Note on the Artwork

A collage is a work of art made by gluing pieces of different materials to a flat surface. I begin my collage by collecting fabric and paper in a variety of textures and colors. When searching for that certain color, I have been known to cut patches out of my husband's shirts or my son's pants. I might decide to rip, scratch, or shred the material also. Sometimes I carefully cut and sew to get that perfect shape. The last step is to bring my illustrations to life with watercolor, embroidery, beads, or that wonderful something that I have found during a nature walk.